D1299808

THE SCIENCE OF LIFE

ANIMAL CLASSIFICATION

by Jenny Fretland VanVoorst

Content Consultant
Tanya Dewey
Animal Diversity Web
University of Michigan

CORE
LIBRARY

Published by ABDO Publishing Company, PO Box 398166, Minneapolis, MN 55439. Copyright © 2014 by Abdo Consulting Group, Inc. International copyrights reserved in all countries. No part of this book may be reproduced in any form without written permission from the publisher. The Core Library™ is a trademark and logo of ABDO Publishing Company.

Printed in the United States of America,
North Mankato, Minnesota
092013
012014

THIS BOOK CONTAINS AT LEAST 10% RECYCLED MATERIALS.

Editor: Arnold Ringstad
Series Designer: Becky Daum

Library of Congress Cataloging-in-Publication Data
Fretland VanVoorst, Jenny, 1972- author.
  Animal classification / by Jenny Fretland VanVoorst.
     pages cm. -- (The science of life)
  Audience: 8-12.
  ISBN 978-1-62403-157-1
1. Animals--Classification--Juvenile literature. I. Title.
  QL352.F74 2014
  590.1'2--dc23

                            2013031884

Photo Credits: Anna Segeren/Shutterstock Images, cover, 1; Dariush M/ Shutterstock Images, 4; Elena Efimova/Shutterstock Images, 7; Christian Musat/ Shutterstock Images, 9; Alexander Roslin, 11; Catalin Petolea/Shutterstock Images, 14; Shutterstock Images, 17, 33, 38; skynetphoto/Shutterstock Images, 20; Red Line Editorial, 22, 39; iStockphoto/Thinkstock, 22 (top left), 22 (bottom left), 22 (bottom middle), 42 (top), 43; Ysbrand Cosijn/Shutterstock Images, 22 (top right); Hamik/Shutterstock Images, 22 (bottom right); Fuse/Thinkstock, 24; Digital Vision/ Thinkstock, 28, 45; De Agostini/SuperStock, 31; Adam J/Shutterstock Images, 34; Digital Vision/Thinkstock, 39; Biosphoto/SuperStock, 42 (bottom)

CONTENTS

CHAPTER ONE

ORGANIZING THE ANIMALS

Shrimp and spiders, ostriches and octopuses, goldfish and gorillas, people and penguins. On the surface these creatures appear to be very different. Some have scales, some have feathers, and others have fur. But all of these creatures have one very important thing in common. They are all members of the animal kingdom.

Millions of types of animals are found in nature. In order to study them better, scientists have divided them into many different categories.

The world is filled with many animals. Some, such as dogs, are familiar to us. But many others may seem strange. Some haven't even been discovered yet. Earth is amazingly rich with life. With so many kinds of animals in the world, scientists need ways to tell one animal from another. Zoologists, scientists who study animals, use an organizing system called taxonomy. Taxonomy organizes animals into groups based on how they are related to each other. Each separate kind of animal is known as a species.

Taxonomy in Your Closet

To understand taxonomy, imagine a closet filled with clothes. There are winter coats and raincoats. There are shorts and dress pants, T-shirts and

Unknown Species

Scientists have classified approximately 2 million species of animals on Earth. But they believe that only a small percentage of Earth's animals have been discovered. In fact, scientists estimate the actual number of animal species may be 30 million.

We see some species of animals every day, but others
have never been seen by human eyes.

sweaters. There are hats, swimsuits, and shoes for every kind of activity. How do you organize these very different pieces of clothing?

You could start by organizing the clothing by season. Spring and summer clothes would go on one side, and autumn and winter clothes would go on the other. Then you might organize by occasion, color, pattern, or material. Now you can tell your friend how your closet is organized. When you ask him to grab the blue cotton T-shirt, he'll know exactly how to find it.

Zoologists use taxonomy in a similar way. Taxonomy assigns each animal a scientific name. For example, *Canis lupus familiaris* refers to domesticated dogs. Special names are also used for groups of animals. If a zoologist is talking about all kinds of dogs, including wolves and coyotes, she would use the name *Canidae*. This is the animal family that includes all kinds of dogs.

Dogs, foxes, and wolves are all included in Canidae.

Scientists and Taxonomy

Swedish scientist Carolus Linnaeus was one of the first scientists to use taxonomy. In 1735 he wrote a book in which he organized nature into categories. Linnaeus started with three categories that he called kingdoms. One kingdom was for animals, one was for plants, and the third was for rocks and crystals. Each kingdom was then divided into more categories.

As later scientists learned more about living things, they changed the categories and added new ones. Because modern taxonomy includes only living things, scientists removed Linnaeus's kingdom of rocks and crystals. They added kingdoms for fungi, bacteria, and single-celled organisms called protists. The taxonomy of living things will always be a work in progress as scientists make new discoveries. One major system of taxonomy used today has five kingdoms: Animalia, Plantae, Fungi,

Other Kingdoms

You are probably familiar with many kinds of animals and plants. But what about the other kingdoms? If you've seen mushrooms in the woods or mold on a piece of fruit, you've seen members of the Fungi kingdom. The Protista kingdom includes tiny single-celled organisms. One example is giardia, which can infect humans and cause illness. Kingdom Monera is made up of bacteria and certain types of algae.

Linnaeus is often called the father of modern taxonomy.

Protista, and Monera. The largest of these kingdoms is the animal kingdom.

So what is an animal, anyway? Most animals share a few features. They are all made of more than one cell. Most are able to move around. They eat other organisms to survive. To really understand what makes up the animal kingdom, we need to look even deeper—into the further divisions that make up the animal kingdom.

In the introduction to his 1735 book *Systema Naturae*, Carolus Linnaeus wrote about the scientific importance of naming and organizing things:

> All that is useful to man originates from. . . natural objects; hence the industry of mining or metallurgy; plant-industry or agriculture and horticulture; animal husbandry, hunting and fishing. . . .
>
> The first step in wisdom is to know the things themselves; this notion consists in having a true idea of the objects; objects are distinguished and known by classifying them methodically and giving them appropriate names. Therefore, classification and name-giving will be the foundation of our science.

Source: Carolus Linnaeus. Systema Naturae. KTH. Royal Institute of Technology, 1735. Web. Accessed August 7, 2013.

Consider Your Audience

Review this passage closely. Consider how you would adapt it for a different audience, such as your parents, your principal, or your younger friends. Write a blog post conveying this same information for the new audience. How does your new approach differ from the original text and why?

CHAPTER TWO

LET'S LOOK AT PHYLA

Kingdom Animalia is the largest of the kingdoms. Below that there are several more levels of division that help scientists classify animals. Each level describes a smaller group of more closely related species. The first of these is called a phylum. The animal kingdom has more than 30 phyla. Phyla are organized around a common evolutionary ancestor. Some animals that don't seem to look very

Chickens, sheep, and people all belong to the animal kingdom.

similar belong to the same phylum because they have evolved in different directions from a similar ancestor. Let's look at some of the more familiar phyla: annelids, arthropods, mollusks, and chordates.

Annelids

You may not recognize the word *annelid*, but you would certainly recognize the animals. Of the 35 phyla in the animal kingdom, nine are made up of animals commonly known as worms because of their shape. Of these, the phylum Annelida contains the worms most familiar to us. *Annelid* means "little ring." The word refers to the segments, or parts, that make up the bodies of worms in this group. This phylum contains

Earthworms are some of the best-known members of the annelid phylum.

several thousand species. Earthworms are annelids. So are leeches. Compared with other creatures in the animal kingdom, worms are very simple animals. They don't have brains. They burrow through dirt, taking in soil through one end of their bodies and removing it through the other end. Earthworms are important to farmers. They churn up the soil as they burrow and eat. Their activity and waste loosen and enrich the soil, making it better for growing crops.

Arthropods

You may think of spiders, flies, centipedes, scorpions, and ticks as bugs. But zoologists call them arthropods. They are animals in the phylum Arthropoda. More than 1 million animal species are classified as arthropods, making it the largest group of animals. In fact, there are more species of arthropod than all other species of animal put together!

Arthropods are covered by hard protective outer structures called exoskeletons. Your skeleton is inside your body, but an arthropod's skeleton is on the outside. These animals can move only the parts of their body that are jointed in their exoskeletons. The word *arthropod* means "jointed foot."

All arthropods have many jointed limbs. They use these limbs to walk or swim. Some also use them to feed themselves or to mate. Arthropod limbs always come in pairs. One side of the body is the same as the other. This is called bilateral symmetry.

Arthropod bodies are divided into segments, or parts, that are connected to one another like train cars. The segments can be very similar or very different. Most of a millipede's segments have two legs. A lobster has several segments, each one with a different purpose.

Most arthropods live on land. Some, such as crayfish, shrimp, and crabs, live in the ocean. These ocean arthropods share some similarities with the bugs we know on land. Look at a picture of a lobster and compare it with a picture of a scorpion. Do you see the similarities?

Clades

As scientists learn more about animals, they find new ways to classify them. Scientists once classified animals mostly based on physical similarity. Now they prefer to group animals based on common ancestors. These groupings by ancestor are called clades.

The world's largest millipede measures more than 15 inches (38 cm) long.

Both have large claws compared to the rest of their bodies. That's why these seemingly different animals belong to the same phylum.

Mollusks

The phylum *Mollusca*, meaning "soft," includes animals such as oysters and clams. These two animals look very similar to each another. Like most mollusks, both have a hard shell. But octopuses and squid are also mollusks. Unlike oysters and clams, they don't have hard outer shells. Instead, they have soft, pulpy bodies. They also have eight legs. Other mollusks, such as slugs, have no shell at all.

So how did scientists decide oysters and octopuses belonged together in phylum Mollusca? Zoologists studied the cells and organs of snails, slugs, and other mollusks and concluded that they share a common ancestor. They found that slugs are very similar to snails, except that slugs lack a shell. As scientists learn more about how various animal species are related, they make changes to the taxonomy.

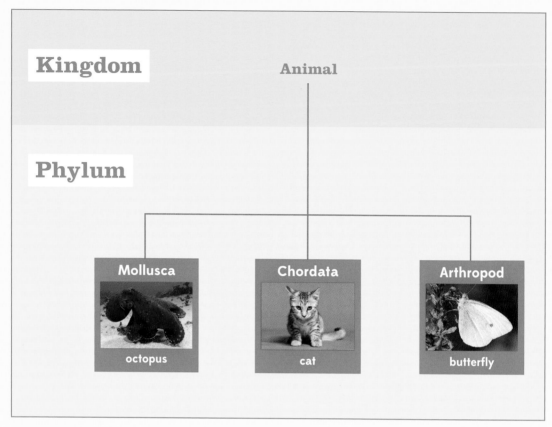

Kingdom — Animal

Phylum

Mollusca — octopus

Chordata — cat

Arthropod — butterfly

Animal Phyla

This diagram shows several of the phyla in the animal kingdom. After reading about phyla and looking at the diagram, can you think of any other animals that might belong to these phyla? Check your guesses at the library or on the Internet.

Chordates

Human beings like you are animals too. You don't have an exoskeleton like an arthropod or a shell like a mollusk. Your body isn't tube-shaped like an annelid.

So what are you? Human beings belong to the phylum Chordata. The members of this phylum include some of the most intelligent species in the animal kingdom.

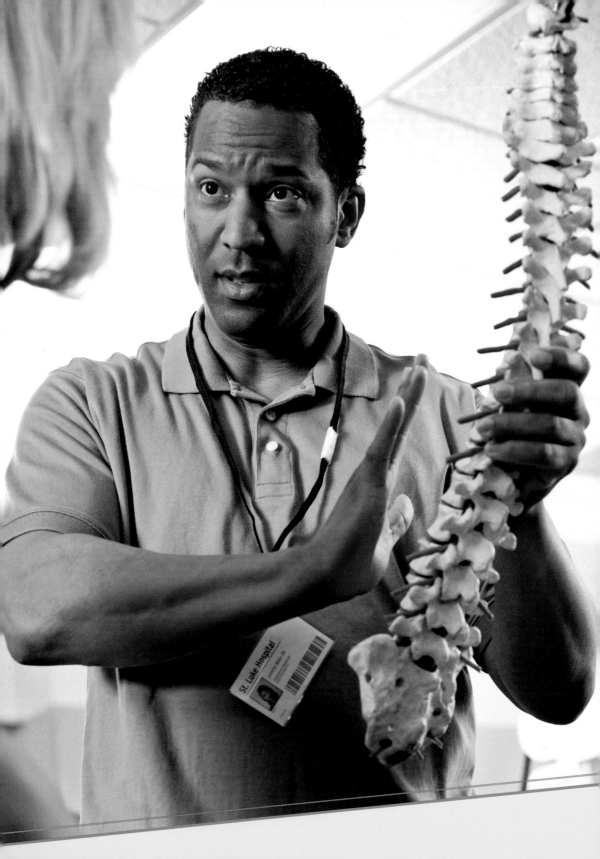

CHAPTER THREE

A CLOSER LOOK AT CHORDATES

What do you have in common with a seagull, a snake, a sheep, and a salamander? You all are members of the phylum Chordata. Though you are very different in many important ways, you are grouped together because you share one important characteristic: you all were born with notochords. When you grew up, your notochord became your backbone.

Vertebrates, members of the phylum Chordata, all have backbones.

Reach around to the middle of your back. Can you feel your vertebrae, the bones that make up your backbone? These bones mean you are a vertebrate. Animals with backbones are called vertebrates. Animals without backbones are invertebrates.

Together these bones create a protective structure that surrounds your spinal cord, a complex rope of nerves that carries messages from your brain to the rest of your body and back again. The backbone also helps hold the body upright. It serves as an anchor for other bones and muscles that help your skeleton move.

Notochords

The name *Chordata* refers to a structure called the notochord. This stiff yet flexible structure is present in the embryos of all chordates. In most chordates, a backbone eventually replaces the notochord. But some chordates keep the notochord. The snakelike lamprey is one chordate that is not a vertebrate. It has a notochord but no backbone.

The phylum Chordata is split into different classes. Some of the more familiar ones are Amphibia, which includes frogs, and Reptilia, which contains reptiles and birds. Birds and reptiles often look very different from each other, but their common ancestors place them in the same class. The class Mammalia includes mammals such as cats, rats, bats, kangaroos, and you!

Amphibians

Frogs, salamanders, toads, and newts are just four of the 7,000 kinds of animals that make up the class Amphibia. The word *amphibian* means "two lives." These animals live a double life—one in water and one on land. For example, most frogs are born from eggs laid in the water. They start life as tadpoles with no legs. Tadpoles use their tails to swim and take in oxygen from the water through their gills. As they grow into frogs, their tails are replaced by legs. Their gills become lungs, allowing frogs to breathe air and live on land.

Amphibians spend part of their lives in water and part on land.

Frogs and their close relatives, toads, make up almost 90 percent of the animal class Amphibia. The other 10 percent includes salamanders, newts, and animals called caecilians. Caecilians look very different from the other members of their class. They have a wormlike appearance. But like other amphibians, caecilians evolved from a common ancestor that lived millions of years ago.

Fish

Fish are chordates too. All fish have gills, live in water, and are vertebrates with backbones. Fish are some of the most ancient species on Earth. Many fish have not changed much over millions of years.

Reptiles

Reptilia comes from a Latin word meaning "to creep." There are more than 10,000 species of reptile. Most of these have four legs, although snakes have no legs at all. Most reptiles, including snakes, turtles, and crocodiles, lay eggs. Their eggs are protected by a thin membrane that allows the eggs to expand as the reptile inside grows. Thanks to this protective membrane, reptiles were the first animals that were able to grow to enormous sizes. In fact, these huge reptiles, which you know as dinosaurs, ruled the planet for many millions of years.

Most of today's reptiles cannot change their own body temperature. They rely on the weather to warm them up or cool them down. For example, a lizard might lie in the sun to warm up and sit in the shade to cool down. A warmer body temperature enables an animal to be more active. That is why reptiles are most often found in warm places.

Birds

It may seem surprising, but the sparrow perched outside your window shares an ancestor with the snake slithering through the grass below. Fossils of the first known bird, Archaeopteryx, show that birds, reptiles, and dinosaurs share a common ancestor. Birds lay eggs like reptiles, but instead of scales they are covered with feathers. There are more than 8,500 species of bird, and most of them can fly.

Archaeopteryx was a prehistoric animal that lived alongside dinosaurs. It was an early link between birds and other reptiles.

Birds once belonged to their own class, Aves. But today, scientists classify birds as reptiles because they are so closely related.

Almost every part of a bird's body is designed to help it fly. From the smallest hummingbird to the largest eagle, bird skeletons are made of hollow

EXPLORE ONLINE

The focus in Chapter Three is on chordates. The Web site below also deals with these organisms. As you know, every source is different. How is the information given in the Web site different from the information in this chapter? What information is the same? How do the two sources present information differently? What can you learn from this Web site?

Animal Classification Games
www.mycorelibrary.com/animal-classification

bones. This reduces the weight of their bodies and makes it easier for them to stay in the air. Unlike many of their fellow reptiles, birds can control their own body temperature. This helps them maintain a constant body temperature and allows them to stay active no matter the weather outside. It enables birds to live in a wide variety of climates, including Antarctica, the coldest place on Earth.

Penguins are specially adapted to live in their extremely cold environment.

CHAPTER FOUR

SO WHO ARE YOU?

So what makes a mammal? Mammals are vertebrates. They have hair or fur, and they are the only group of animals that produce milk to feed their young. Almost all mammals give birth to live young, rather than laying eggs as reptiles and birds do. Adult mammals care for their young until they are old enough to live on their own. Like birds, mammals generate their own heat to

One key feature of mammals is that they feed milk to their babies.

35

maintain a constant body temperature. Hippos and horses, deer and dolphins, and whales and wombats are all mammals. You are a mammal too.

The more than 4,000 species that make up the class Mammalia include some of the most intelligent organisms on Earth. Their large brains enable some species to solve problems and adapt to their surroundings. Mammals have backbones that can support large, active, sturdy bodies. With hair or fur to keep them warm, mammals are able to live in very cold places.

Mammals are divided into 28 orders. Order is the division below class. Animals in the same order share similar behaviors and physical characteristics.

Monotremes

Most mammals bear live young, but not all do. An order of animals called monotremes lay eggs. A platypus is a monotreme. So is the echidna, an animal also known as a spiny anteater. When the eggs hatch, however, both the platypus and echidna nurse their young like other mammals.

The largest of these is Rodentia, with more than 2,000 species of rats, squirrels, mice, and chipmunks. Cats are in the order Carnivora. This order also includes wolves, bears, and seals. Whales and dolphins are in the order Cetacea. It may seem surprising that whales and dolphins are mammals too. But they share the feature that all mammals have in common—the mothers feed their babies milk.

Classifying You

So who are you? You are an animal, a chordate, and a mammal. You are also a primate. The order Primates includes monkeys, apes, and lemurs, as well as human beings. Modern humans belong to one of the families within the Primates order, Hominidae. Family is the group below class. Organisms in the same family are even more closely related than organisms in the same class. Other animals in the Hominidae family include gorillas, bonobos, and chimpanzees. Humans belong to a genus within the Hominidae family called *Homo*. This group includes ancient people that lived

Bonobos are among the closest primate relatives to humans.

alongside modern humans but later died out. Finally, modern humans belong to the species *sapiens*. In taxonomy, animals are usually named by their two most specific classifications—genus and species.

Kingdom: Animal

Phylum: Chordates

Class: Mammals

Order: Primates

Family: Hominids

Genus: *Homo*

Species: *sapiens*

The Human Species

This list shows the taxonomy of *Homo sapiens* from kingdom down to species. After reading Chapter Four and looking at this outline of human taxonomy, where would chimpanzees and lemurs split off from *Homo sapiens*? Which is more closely related to people?

When you say *Homo sapiens*, scientists know you are referring to modern humans.

Homo sapiens are the most intelligent organisms on Earth. Compared to the size of the rest of the body, humans have enormous brains. You can use both logic and imagination. You can come up with new ideas and solve complex problems. You can speak, write, teach, and learn. Working together, human beings have created great civilizations, including the one you're a part of right now.

The animal kingdom is large, fascinating, and diverse. And yet, from the largest elephant to the smallest ant, every creature has its own special place. Organizing this life helps us understand it. Understanding helps us care about it. And caring about it helps us act to protect Earth's life.

Renowned scientist Edward O. Wilson believes that as the most advanced members of the animal kingdom, human beings have a responsibility to preserve the planet:

> *We are the brain of the biosphere. We are the ones that finally, after 4.5 billion years of evolution—that's what it took to get to where we are—actually developed enough power, reasoning power, to see what's happening, to understand the history that created us and to realize almost too late what we're doing. So in the sense that we are something new under the sun and on the Earth. . . we're the ones that can destroy the world. No other single species ever had anything like that power. We have the power to destroy the world, the living world. And we also have the knowledge to avoid doing it.*

Source: Edward O. Wilson. "Interview with Bill Moyers." PBS. PBS, July 6, 2007. Web. Accessed August 7, 2013.

Back It Up

Do you agree with Wilson's statement? First write a couple of sentences describing the point the author is making. Then write down two or three pieces of evidence from your own experience that could be used to support his claim.

HOW SCIENTISTS STUDY ANIMAL CLASSIFICATION

Fossil Studies

Scientists use fossils to gather information on animals that lived long ago. This is useful information for taxonomy because it helps scientists make connections between these early animals and those that are alive now. Fossils have helped scientists make connections between dinosaurs and early birds. They help scientists understand how different animals have evolved over time.

The discovery of Archaeopteryx fossils was key in making the link between dinosaurs and birds.

Dissection

Scientists sometimes practice dissection to learn more about an animal. Dissection is cutting into the dead body of an animal for the purpose of studying it. New species are being discovered all the time. In these cases, scientists may dissect an animal to find out about its anatomy. For example, they would want to find out how its digestive system works, what its skeleton and organs look like, and if it has any unusual features that may link it to other known animals.

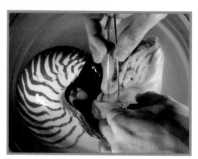

Dissection in science labs can help improve our understanding of how animals are related to each other.

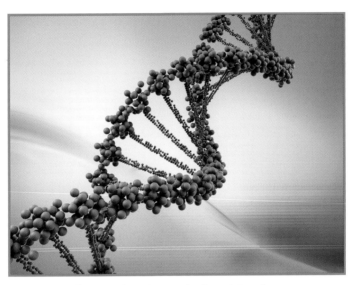

DNA can show scientists relationships between animals that would be impossible to figure out based on simply comparing how they look.

DNA Comparisons

Deoxyribonucleic acid (DNA) is essentially a recipe for an animal. It is a chemical located in the cells of an organism that includes information about that organism. It determines whether an animal has hair or scales, wings or arms, and two legs or twenty. Zoologists look at an animal's DNA to learn more about its ancestry. By comparing an animal's DNA to that of other animals, zoologists can learn about how the animal evolved.

STOP AND THINK

Surprise Me

Chapters Two and Three discuss animals that are grouped together based on a common ancestor. These groups can be interesting and surprising. After reading this book, what two or three facts stood out to you about these unusual groupings? Write a few sentences about each fact. Why did you find them surprising?

Take a Stand

This book discusses the ways zoologists classify creatures in the kingdom Animalia. We classify people as well—for example, by physical appearance, profession, lifestyle, and so on. In which ways can classifying human beings be helpful? In which ways can it be harmful? Write a short essay explaining your opinion. Make sure to give reasons for your opinion, and facts and details that support those reasons.

Tell the Tale

This book discusses the way the animal kingdom is organized. Write a few paragraphs that tell about how you would classify a new animal you have discovered. Start by creating an animal. What does it look like? Does it have fur or feathers? Does it swim or fly? What existing animals are similar? Be sure to set the scene, develop a sequence of events, and offer a conclusion.

Why Do I Care?

We use classification to make our everyday lives easier. Can you think of an example of how you might use classification at school? Use your imagination!

GLOSSARY

algae
simple plants that often grow in water

bacteria
tiny organisms made of a single cell

cell
the smallest part that makes up an organism

domesticated
tamed and kept as a pet or a farm animal

embryo
an organism at any time before full development, birth, or hatching

enriches
improves the quality of

gills
breathing organs found in many marine organisms that take in dissolved oxygen from water

limbs
arms or legs

zoologist
a scientist who studies animals

LEARN MORE

Books

Arlon, Penelope. *First Animal Encyclopedia*. New York: Dorling Kindersley, 2004.

Spelman, Lucy. *National Geographic Animal Encyclopedia*. Washington, DC: National Geographic, 2012.

Web Links

To learn more about animal classification, visit ABDO Publishing Company online at **www.abdopublishing.com**. Web sites about animal classification are featured on our Book Links page. These links are routinely monitored and updated to provide the most current information available. Visit **www.mycorelibrary.com** for free additional tools for teachers and students.

INDEX

ABOUT THE AUTHOR

Jenny Fretland VanVoorst is a writer and editor of books for young people. She lives in Minneapolis, Minnesota, with her husband, Brian, and their two wonderful pets.